THE WHOLE FIELD STILL
MOVING INSIDE IT

THE WHOLE FIELD STILL

MOVING INSIDE IT

by

MOLLY BASHAW

WINNER OF THE 2013 WASHINGTON PRIZE

THE WORD WORKS
WASHINGTON, D.C.

FIRST EDITION, FIRST PRINTING
The Whole Field Still Moving Inside It
Copyright © 2014 Molly Bashaw

  The Word Works, PO Box 42164, Washington, DC 20015
  wordworksbooks.org editor@wordworksbooks.org

Cover art: Kathleen Laraia McLaughlin, 1999, photograph.
Author photograph: Melinda P. Dolan
Book design: Susan Pearce Design
Library of Congress Control Number: 2013916632
International Standard Book Number: 978-0-915380-89-3

ACKNOWLEDGMENTS

Thanks to the editors of the following journals in which some of the poems first appeared:

Beloit Poetry Journal: "Posing Nude for Andrew Wyeth," "Music Box," "Josephine"; *Comstock Review*: "On Writing Down the Farm Words"; *Crazyhorse*: "Every Time I Have Never Been Here Before," "Letter to a Farm," "There Were No Mirrors in That Farmhouse"; *River Styx*: "A Talk with Chagall"; *Salamander*: "Letter to a Farm," "There's a Liturgical Sound to Our Names for Her Stomachs"; *Small Farmers' Journal*: "The Day Emily Dickinson Helped My Father Build a Small House in Vermont," "Letter to a Farm"; *Sow's Ear Poetry Review*: "The Syntax of the Barn," "In the Dark These Animals Are Just Bells," "Luminous Terrain," "The End of Myth," "For Kevin Ford, Hand Shearer."

I would also like to express my deepest gratitude to:

James Longenbach, Lee Sharkey, Cathy and Austin Kodra, Austin Smith, and Peter Watson, for giving this collection a good read.

Borders Books, the New York State Summer Writers Institute, the Bread Loaf Writers' Conference, Phillips Exeter Academy, and Elias Kulukundis, for their generous support.

The judges and editors at The Word Works, especially Nancy White— for all your help, starting on the day you drove up the long hilly road to the farm and ate with us and then braved the outhouse.

And Audrey Gerkin of Pickpocket Farm, Andreas Maier and Marion Kaspar of Hof Honigmilch, and Elizabeth Hendrix of Sunny Hill Farm, for patiently hosting me while I tried my hands at farming.

for my mother
and for my father

THE WHOLE FIELD STILL MOVING INSIDE IT

JOSEPHINE

My great-grandmother was a farmer and a pianist in a silent movie theater. When she died, she left me a music dictionary. On the first page she had written in pencil:

Modulation: Under the cow, one note changes milk-on-pail
to milk-on-milk.

Staccato: Write music with cornmeal on your belly skin.
Invite the chickens.

Polyrhythmic: Night, August. Crickets in the marsh.

Pianissimo: Maple sap rains in the maple woods.

Perfect pitch: When the pumpkin grows, hold it to your ear.

MUSIC BOX

I was born of a carpenter and a seamstress.

Father built stilts for himself. Stars held his waist
like a skirt. He sang opera.

Mother sewed slippers to fit the stilt tips.

They were charged with juggling
fire too close to the sky

and decided to try their hands
at farming:
mother knit me a sweater out of popcorn,
flour corn,
dent corn, sweet corn, flint corn.

Father milked the house cat.

We sat on riding saddles
in front of the fireplace. Horseless.

Wood from the old piano, hacked in thirds,
burnt wild blossoms of sparks.

INHERITANCE

My father has built a chicken coop.
Blond wood on the west field, below it purple stones.
Each hen in her nesting box.

No holes: no rat
will suck the whites and yolk.
Pocket full of nails and pencil,

pocket full of corn,
hole in his pocket,
feathers in his hat.

To me he offers all of it—
the disk harrow,
the row of plows, the weathervane's

East, bent onto South.
The barn is held together by hardened leather reins.
The scythe hides its blade in its sleeve.

If I want it I must come to it
a warm horse,
a field of warm grain,

trade one line for three magic beans.

LUMINOUS TERRAIN

Out to feed the chickens a leftover bone,
—green-black ripple of chickens,
getting closer and closer to the bone—
I see the smaller birds leave suddenly,
still in the shape of the tree.
Their shadows race across the field
with horsehair blown from the currycomb.
Only the Highland cattle have always known slowly
to pace in the shape of a five-leafed clover.
All evening I practice looking into their deep
black hides through the cow-licked briskets to their hearts.
All evening I stand at the window.
A candle looks at me that way, too—
this light that once flew, this light made by bees.

Morning, rainy day
in the granary. In an arc of grain
and light, grain is falling into grain.
Inside one grain it is last summer still:
the white farmhouse curtains blow
free, then fall back. Inside one grain
it is the summer before that: two deer
at the edge of meadow recede
into the grove like pulled ropes.
Sack for sack I carry it
into the room with the tin roof
where cats bat a chewed mouse,
bin to bin. Have mercy, I ask,
but not of them. Of memory.

A TALK WITH CHAGALL

I confess:
I have drunk ice-cold water from a trough.

I have taken a cow's teat into my mouth, the cowbell so silent
it rang through the body into the milk.

The cow the world.

The cow feeding my family yoghurt for ten years!

My mother came apart and spread herself onto the cabbages,
sugarhouse vapors settled, dirt fell up,
her hands in the grain bins, her hands in the trees.

Behind this night,
she said,

there is another night.

*

The cow has many stomachs with beautiful names:
rumen, omasum, abomasum, reticulum.
And I have many hearts:
one for my father running the whetting stone
along the scythe, one for the apple blossoms falling like snow,
one for those nights he milked her, his head rested on the fetus inside,
the eyes of the compost blinking to let off steam.
And yet, one single green eye stayed shut.

What is farm?
The bones of trees oiled with honey,
the castrated pigs hurling shouts at my father.

We wear potatoes on our fingers,
we braid garlic and onions with our hair.

The vetch invites the scythe to dance.

*

When the blind Amish man came to our farm,
the trees stepped aside, the barn opened its door
for him, horses moved carefully.

He did not need his white cane,
he did not need his guide dog trained by the monks,
he did not need a miracle to heal him.

The barn was blind, the horses were blind.
The trees were blind, the kittens were blind.

Commissioned to make new harness and yokes
for the draft-horses, he walked around and under them,
talking softly, taking measurements
with his voice.

*

I arrived in the world amid the colors of slaughter—

they fell blacker and whiter until the world
was a photograph of itself.

And who would have believed the inside of the pig slit open:
its pure fable of no good and no evil,

the hard stomach, the lungs emptying,
the heart its own animal?

Who would have believed the roan mares, come to drink?
They put their noses in, the level sinks.

The woodpile rests on its elbows.
The rafters breathe,
the cat jumps, upside down, through that ribcage like a bat
as it is supposed to.

*

The goat and my mother:
it rests its bearded chin on her head.
She rests her chin on its flank,
it rests its hoof on her thigh,
she rests her hands on its horns,
it rests its eyes on her eyes.
She rests her eyes in its milk.

You would think
someone watched over these scenes with a whip made of wheat.
You would think so soft breathed by grain.

*

The empty grain silo is my double bass,
my thousand chickens carrying their silent eggs.
What bow, what hair of what horse will rub rosin
across that hollow place where grain once was,
what stroke will tell that story that starts with a disk of ferns
and ends with a disk of dipper, the handle
attached to the ladle I know is there, too?

Who will talk like an old man
of the cow the goat the milk
the cow the goat the milk
until these are not symbols?

The scent of hay the workhorses the troughs
the scent of hay the workhorses the troughs.

You live by them as you did then, in repetition,
one foot on the house, one foot on the barn,
conducting the world in your too-small purple coat.

It is not sound you are after, but sound before sound,
sound inside sound, sound after sound.
Something like color,
the grain come down to cover you.

*

The head closer to the ground, hinges in the hip,
we're bent down
to hear songs on the other sides of this surface.

That is why animals hang their heads low,
the chickens scratch.
That is what is meant by graze, grace, grass.

The leaves wine-colored, blue. The pigs drinking.
We stand with them at the trough,
having just molded them out of clay,
having just molded ourselves, our rumps, our big toes.

Bending together this moment,
our eyes meet in the reflection of trough water,
the pig inside us looking at us inside the pig.

That is what is meant by face, façade, facet.

Come pig, we will go home now, where is your home?
You are not from the barn?
There are rafters there that will make you weep.
You don't exist?
There is grain there that will tell all the tales.
There is a clothesline there that has no ends.
We are there, poking potatoes in the coals, up on the hill, looking for nuts.
We are raising our glasses to cider.

*

When the rooster crows you must go back to the farm.
You will hear it, eating eggs, eggs inside you,
eggs called home by the rooster.

When he calls you, you may go.
Bring him something, a piece of tree, a blue hat,
a sliver of moon.

Bring him your eggs and be generous.
Bring him your feathers, but go,
go now, board the ship due east, due west,

the farm is everywhere, a constellation
you can see
when you look just to the side of it.

*

Even now the cow holds my coat for me,
she holds the umbrella, the shoe horn.

She holds the coat for the whole joyful sad town.
Sometimes she is a priest, sometimes a rabbi,
sometimes she is God, sometimes she teaches us
we are not as far away from the farm as we thought.

Let me kneel at you once more,
I will imagine the earth inside you
beginning with the grass,

then an owl very still in a tree, its breathing audible.
Let me follow you, cattle, come
Boss, come Bess, come sallow-eyed Jersey,
come Charolais, Holstein, and old Swiss-Brown,

I will lick your fingers with my long rough tongue.

WHO WILL REMEMBER WHAT THIS LOOKED LIKE FROM ABOVE?

My ancestors were farmers, a prison guard, an antique dealer, a logger, a sawyer, the owner of a general store, a blacksmith, a weaver, a mother, a mother, a mother, a mother. One fourth of them were buried in Massachusetts, in ground that later became the floor of Quabbin Reservoir, and were moved to a nearby cemetery when the Swift River Valley was flooded to create Boston's main water source. The few people who remember those towns—Enfield, Prescott, Greenwich, Dana— are over eighty years old. When I visit family still living in the area, we hike to Quabbin Hill, what was then probably more of a mountain. We look down onto the water, where the maiden names seem to float up to the surface and blossom into water lilies. A man on a boat is fishing above Enfield—his sinker reaches down to where Josephine once played for Buster Keaton's *The Cameraman*, her face lit by the stand lamp clamped to the piano, the cue sheet indicating running upstairs, then down, minor key, major key. Had she ever, on a Sunday afternoon after the matinee, I wonder, run with the antique dealer up this hill and looked down, too? And were they standing underneath this same tree? Did they kiss, or did he whisper to her earring first, words that made her soften in her dress? Did an ancestor of that hawk soaring now, soar above them—and catch their words in its wings?

THE SYNTAX OF THE BARN

Held in place by the two pigs
strung up inside it, opened, emptied, intestines
on the floor.

The ninety-degree angles softened
by spider webs.

Holes in the rafters filled with swallows.

If the chickens got up from their eggs
too early, I knew it would disappear.

All summer, sleeping with cats in nests.
The dream in my father's voice

a part of the shape of the dust and dripping blood,
the floorboards' nails worn shiny.

The grain held the barn here. Pig slop and water
frozen in the tubs; each birthing ewe,
each testicle held the barn here.

The animals were a wall,
the voice was a wall,
the animals were a wall,
the voice was a wall.

On the roof
we ate new carrots from a bucket,

rolling the stubs up to the peak
to see if they would make it.

LOWING

A week before Christmas
our largest Scotch Highland bull
is down in the round pen, the cow
in the paddock by the house.
They send heat through the air,

calling for two days across the barren pasture.

And even this poem, which, at first, seems to want to,
cannot keep Aurochs from jumping
two split rail fences, taking quickly
the position Iris prepares for him,
their hocks certain of that stance.

RÉSUMÉ

We made wallets out of old boots, burped

the kombucha, culled dill.

Lice walked like flowers over the trellis of our bodies.

The boys wore hand-me-down dresses.

We lanced the horse's abscess ourselves, trimmed

the sheep dingle, then knitted

with those fingers, the holes the size of sparrows' feet.

We rubbed the butternut squashes until we all agreed

we could feel them when they were gone.

We wanted to see who would come, who would sing along, and so

we shared this meal.

Before I went to sleep, I put a red onion under my pillow.

THERE WERE NO MIRRORS IN THAT FARMHOUSE

Peacocks screamed us into ourselves.

In wood, in wool, we welled up, about to appear.

We could not tell if our faces were most ours

in the yellow hawthorn, the cornhusk, or milk.

In bonfires we stayed the same, in moss we aged.

We called out to ourselves like one black ox

braying across the pasture to the other black ox.

And when the wind rose at night we heard

the barn swallows gather and land inside us.

Kerosene lamps threw our bodies onto the walls.

Deer in the dogwood lee breathed us to sleep.

As if this were not enough to keep us there,

we tied ourselves to the dun mare, we held on

to wooden handles, we covered ourselves

with wool and buttons, saying: my stonewall,

my dark barn, my marmot, my ptarmigan,

my tilth, my kiln. We gathered heavy words

until we were full as the silo once full of grain.

When we dreamt of a ghost caught

on the mulberry bush where silkworms chewed

through a shawl, we woke again to clothesline

carrying our stiff pants.

Late evening in the lit barn we brought

the stone-boat to a halt, soft-whistled

our team back into its stall. It must have been

because we had been separating stones

from pebbles from stones so deeply gone

they could not touch the plow, stones

from boulders for our wall, that the hay bale

we threw down from the loft, held together

by two short pieces of twine,

seemed weightless and full of light.

The whole field still moving inside it.

SAYING GRACE

John Clare, I whisper. I have cooked
Swiss chard quiche and a butternut squash
soup. I have made salad with pine nuts
and apples. There's a slice of thick bread
from the brick oven. Or would you prefer
some of the lamb we raised, roasted,
rubbed with honey and fresh mint?
John Clare. Here's butter from Jersey
cream. Would you like a glass
of beer before you carry on your way?
A sandwich for the road, thick
cheddar slices on sourdough loaf?
I've made tea, with echinacea,
John Clare. Take it with you.

THE FUTURE

Below the Canada geese sowing their alphabet into the sky, I sow winter rye cover crop onto the dirt, tilled open, still warm from the summer months. The last tomatoes are only skins now, paper lanterns. One okra petal falls. The patterns I throw must seem random to the geese in their neat V above. My arm makes figure eights, crossing in front of my body, then stays longer on one side, my wrist and hand in vibrato. Sometimes I am the priest who throws out his censer and draws it back, the conductor beating a four-four time, sometimes I am the fly fisherman, drawing in his line, or the child with her hand out the car window, catching wind. I am waving a sparkler. I am throwing next year onto the field.

TALKING WITH THE GEESE ABOUT ART

There is no mystery here, they tell me, guarding
the mailbox from everyone, chasing my nephew
into the house crying. Never, never give up on reality.
Don't put us into your poem, they warn, writing
their own words in black and blue on my shins.
And of course, they are right. We live the same
here, each day, each gray sky illiterate above
the gray barn, the mustard field, the columns
of trees perpendicular to the even wagon tracks.
Surely there is no compensation beyond
small change: the equinox, the cherry.
And what good is metaphor when in old letters
there really are fingers writing, in sweaters, fingers
holding wool? But why, also, geese, have we named you
Blanziflor and Helena? And why is there joy
in lining the brooms in the barn into a row
against the empty stall wall, walking from one side
to the other, or in placing stones into the wheelbarrow?
Why do I see the sheepdogs circle the sheep and think,
compass, magnet, circumference? Why words at all, geese?

PLUCKED CLEAN

I dreamt my sonnet was a Cornish hen,
its gizzard taut with grain and bits of gravel.
I used a paring knife to stop its brain
and cut the sopping head into a shovel.
I scalded it and rubbed the feathers off
and singed with lighted paper feathers left
around the feet that danced and left a whiff
of candle wicks and straw bales in the loft.
One hand inside, one hand around the wings
I found the oviduct, and tiny sacks
beside the crop. The heart. The spleen. The lungs.
I cut and washed its long and slippery neck,
then cooked and ate what tasted good to me.

IN THE DARK THESE ANIMALS ARE JUST BELLS

They come to the sound of the pail

in the grain that becomes the sound

of the grain in the pail. They come

easily, but we must guide ourselves

along the rail of their horn and bone

towards the milk, the milk on the pail,

the milk on the milk foam. And then we

let them go, and then we call them

again, we put on rope, we take off rope,

listening for some essential sound,

like the words held between the workhorse

on the left and the workhorse on the right.

The goats, as they trace the circles

of goats gone, shift, goat by goat,

from this herd to the herd the herd

carries inside the herd, in every hoof

the hot field surrounded by poppies,

in every hoof every field the field ever was.

BLOOD RED

The blackbirds, poison ivy

and grain: everything the goat

had ever seen still twitches

below the strung-up carcass

Andreas undresses, preparing

the meats, but I am still, staring

at this clotting in the blue-green

grass that looks back through me

with the matte eye of paintings

I have known, not leaf-brown,

of wound or birth, not of this

earth. Primary.

It can be broken further only into sound.

GOVERNED BY THE THRUMMING
OF MY MOTHER'S SPINNING WHEEL

and the running of the shuttle
through the warp with the weft
and the binning of the corn
from the bags to the bins
and the bats with the loft
brimming on their breaths
and the sum of the ringing
of the herd running in

the vetch as it's catching
on the snath-swung blade
the stinging of the swarm
by the smell of the stung
the willows singing weeping
to the minnows in the creek
and my father reading cummings
to the tails of the team

the pinning to the stall wall
one ram the other
and the numbing of the frost
on the coq's red comb
the humming birds stringing
their motor through a flower
and no pipes and no plumbing
in the walls of this home

the dinging of the bells
when they're resting on the dung
the corn humming solos
in the silo's silent wood
the ewes lambing hooves,
limbs, tongue,
and the dimming of the drumming
of the coming of that blood.

THE DAY EMILY DICKINSON HELPED MY FATHER
BUILD A SMALL HOUSE IN VERMONT

My father is like that, he wants to build a farm, he starts with the
outhouse. He lives in a tent all year, sanding the moon, staining glass,
pounding out candleholders at a neighbor's forge. One day a car stops
at the edge of fields his cows will someday graze—maybe a flock of
sheep—and out steps Emily Dickinson, hoisting her dress. Pleasure, my
father says, removing his straw hat, taking her hand. She asks for a room
with a window, not too big, *untouched by morning, untouched by noon, rafter
of satin, roof of stone.* My father is scratching his head, looking behind
him up the hill where the forest ends and field rolls out green. Can I
offer you some well water, he asks, I'm still at work on the buildings.
This isn't a motel, won't ever be, but I can give you a piece of shade and
a cool drink. Actually, I've been making that outhouse—can you see it
up there—since April. Emily's sunbonnet covers her face and tight hair;
in the field in a balloon of her black dress she drinks water while my
father hammers nails through the afternoon. Where're you headed, he
yells, but Emily doesn't answer, she is lost in thought. My father is not
offended—in addition to cedar shingles he is now thinking rafter, he is
thinking *satin rafter?*

POSING NUDE FOR ANDREW WYETH

The old wagon became a sexual being

reminding of its history as trees, the wood steamed
and giving way, the wood measured by hands, turned
on a lathe, the wood fitted and driven into place,
the axle under the breast still lithe, the tongue
still reaching out for a team.

*

The sweet bright black flesh of earth
was an ear we listened to

as it listened.
Are you speaking of us, we asked.

In it a scent of rope and garments, carob, the threshing machine.

We held the reins, the fences held the fields' hands,
in them the scent of eggshells, fish, the sea.

Leather stretched taut rubbed on the bit,
the britchen, the bells.
The furrow rushed over
our feet, a wave of sepia milk,

in it the scent of ink and beaks,

the voice of the sky,
the voice of the ground,
the voice of the sky,
the voice of the ground.

O raven, O blackbird, O crow,
we only accused you of what we also were.

*

The honey and the onions spoke:

I am wrapped in my own skin.
I am wrapped low down, around a branch of oak.

I rise up from underground, drawn by the sun.
I was celebrated before they took the comb.

I cast a reddish, purplish hue.
I have been eaten by animals quickly, bursting with bees.

Drying on barn boards, you'd think I was a group of forgotten travelers.
In those hexagons there is perfect memory.

Unwrapping me you might expect a center.
I am a tent built around the scent of a small queen's body.

I am pages of water.
I connect the buckwheat blossoms to each other.

*

Yes, said the grass body,
I carry my psalm in your palm.

*

The logging scoot
used in spring to drag
woods to the mills,

its big wood thighs—pale in that sunlight
that snuck through darkest branches—
pinned together and chained up, the peavey
driven in to rest there,

it told the story of body weight,
dragging nights through mud.

An image we hitched ourselves to and pulled,
an image that pulled us,
an image we hitched ourselves to and pulled,
an image that pulled us.

Though the cord of chopped wood spoke two languages,
one of silver maple trees, one of fire,

it was the language of the stove that saved us,

the iron house,
the ashes we carried from it,

that rocking chair.

*

The doors to the barn were never completely shut, propped
from swinging open by a board, the old wood sagging
and the hinges bent, a wreath of wind in the rafters. The sound
of snow on the roof said to the mouse, fox, or tramp who'd slipped in
through those cracks and found grain and nested in the eaves;

the sound of snow
on the roof said to anyone who listened:

no one possesses the kingdom of dust.

*

A punt in the field quietly going to pieces,
a rowboat next to the grain silo,
one oar left, taking on moss, letting go,
a dory tucked into the eaves of the barn
floating on the sun coming into the hay in the loft
like bright green seawater,

though the only water for miles around
was in the spring-fed trough
and in the spring itself.

The horses shifted their weight to different hooves,
the cat knocked over a clay pot

to the gale of barn swallows.

Rows of old silken women
on the winter cornfield
smiled their two-toothed cobs.

They held brown flags, mauve and beige flags.

The train rushed past.
They said: You are that strong.
The tassels moved in the wind,
singing want

is a delicacy, always, further—
Bear witness.

COMMISSION

for Meghan Martin

Can you write me a poem
about cat fur, she asks?
You know, when
they've just run in
from blackberry bushes?
That stink of skunk
that fades to something
sweet and faint and returns
when they are warm—
or, end of autumn
when they've run in
bushy-tailed from woods,
carrying fox-scent, carrying
coyotes on them,
carrying leaves
and snow, the owl
they watched, the hawk
that soared through
their eyes as they lay
on the old log full of honey?
You can smell the queen
in that fur. Can you make
a poem like this? As long
as the cat's unknown path
at night, as wide as the creek
where the cress
and wild leeks grow, packed
as the mile of stacked hay?
The words could, themselves,
still smell of apple trees
and chewed mice, wood
smoke, old boards,
sheep trails run hard,

silent in the rain.
Make it hold
where it has been
on its skin,
make it bring in
offerings, a half-toad, a
still-live chipmunk.
Make it smell
like the field,
then drag it in, leave it
at the foot of my bed.

HISTORY OF A SWEATER

That summer day my mother walked in woods
collecting bright yellow florets of rag-
wort the copper butterfly also found.
Galls the sun had filled with color fell
from oaks. She gathered them in her shirt, she
carried them from the woods to the garden,
she pulled and braided golden onions. Sheep
pressed their mouths onto pasture, she pushed her
fingers into wool soon Kevin Ford would come
to shear. Soon all of this would be taken, soon
it would seem to have been of one piece I would wear.

FOR KEVIN FORD, HAND SHEARER

who said: *It takes a thousand sheep to start getting it smooth.*

In ewes' shoulders you feel the eskers left by glaciers,
in hooves, the meadow-crows.
You lift your shears

when you are finished turning the flock through your fingers,
as though still conducting after a final curtain call.
Why should you notice the scuttle

of Narragansett and Bourbon Butternut turkeys
or the farm around you that has gone on
while you were working:

the horse, the man, the plow
who have turned the buckwheat fields
from white to bright black?

Wind gusts in sassafras trees
whistle to the Border Leicester sheepdogs,
but you are quiet, piling silence at your feet.

ON WRITING DOWN THE FARM WORDS

The most important mythical figure for us is Sisyphus, my mother told
me, as potatoes rolled out of her hands into a bushel basket. He was
a farmer, she said, which meant he could build a stone wall and could
roll a swarm of bees out of a tree back into its hive. He could slaughter
a lamb with a hammer and knife as my mother could. Nights he mas-
saged the tired muscles, rolling his stone over every contour in the farm's
body. She never said it was punishment.

Sisyphus, too, grieved each time, afterwards,
for the beginning, for the way his stone
had felt in the sun on the first day: the ease

of turning it forwards, as if playing a marble,
before he knew it would roll back down
past the sheep and hollyhocks. I've memorized

the clothesline, the wraparound porch
where a shucked pea once rolled away
through a crack. I can see my mother still,

folding-in the garden, smoke from the coal forge
hovering above her. Like a worm, curled
around a bolt, I recall the harrow, the plow,

the metal shoes of Clydes who used to wait
at the end of each row, slacking their reins,
blinking slowly at my father's chafed hands.

They are gone and still I hold them—
They are the stones most mine. *Alfalfa.*
Swath. Gargot. Umbel. Sod.

HIPPOCRATES PRESCRIBES THE GOATS

Gather them
along the path
at the base of the mountain,
they are carrying milk.

And when you can see inside them
as though into earthenware jugs,
compare everything else
with milk.

Gather them when they run across hard dirt fields,
gather them when they fly like birds into the fallen tree.
Already they have milk you will not find,
squeezing out the last milk.

Hold one in each hand,
you will live there.
When you sit on the hillside
under the apples, they will be watching,
planting their hooves, gathering milk.

You may feel love,
but your love will never be as great
as the milk still inside the goats.
They will wrap you in ribbons of milk.

Gather them, hold each goat to your ear.
They will gather you.
Anchor in that condition
that presses you deeper into the milk,

let the milk enter you,
and when you walk away from the goats, finally,
gather them.

FLY FISHING

Far from the river, between the field of barley
and the unmown meadow, on grass framed
by yellow flowers, you practice throwing the line.
It whips the air to find its place, sometimes
faster than you can see. It falls out in front
of you into the field's face. You forget the fish,
but the afternoon waits patiently, the sheepdog brings
his stick. You throw the line and then the stick,
and when the goats get out you go and gather them,
lift them back over their fence. What holds you
is the line—behind you, in front of you,
its never perfect shapes, gone as they are formed—

THE FIELD IS ARCHAIC AND SOUNDS
LIKE A TRANSLATION

All August I ride on the Clydesdale horse
my father drives, making hay with the scythe
and the fork and the wagon. People stop their cars
along the road to see the bright field taken
by hand. They point and they stare. Look, they say,
that is how people used to live. And then they pull
their children, before they are finished, away
from the field. Don't go, I want to say, listen
to the story passed to us in the milk pod, listen
and you can still hear the rangale of deer and the doles
of doves, the clowder of cats. Here we are yeomen.
The letter A still walks on its head, a horned ox,
the C will roll into a camel, the H holds them
in its pens. Here you learn Phoenician. You find
haver in your oat, you touch the spanged cow,
the harrow and shoat. It is awkward and hard
but stay and carry with us this field across the fields.

LEARNING TO READ

I left my book out on the field in the rain

but back in the dark to look for it

could not remember which patch of vetch,

which blades of grass. I ran my fingers over

a zucchini, wet eggplants,

the black currants.

In the distance a light in the barn still on—

my father in there, my father

who'd once spelled the word *goat* for me on the dirt

using goat shit

so I would never forget. My father,

who had wanted to write an opera,

rocking in the barn,

reads poems to the team

so they will learn the smallest left and right of his voice.

I still have not found my book

but I can smell those horses through the dark:

I could put them into my mouth and say them.

SWINGING FROM FROST'S BIRCHES,
THOUGH WE HAD OUR OWN

And now I wish I had paid more attention to the rhubarb.
Shakespeare could have come to the farm. Bach,
to the silo. We could have learned to make compote from my mother.
I learned to read but I did not learn to read the rhubarb. I crouched down,
reading, as though weeding, when my mother walked by
with the leeks. Why did I not listen to the rocks and learn
to drive the team? Why was I not reading the bucks
and skinning a lamb, tying knots? Is there no authority
in Cary's hill, no culture in the back field
where my mother feeds her queen?

MASTERS

Between the wet clothes,
I hang them on the line:
a shirt, a poem, a sock, a poem,
and then the long rooms of cotton sheets

the wind opens.

If nothing dries today,
let it wait with sparrows,
and I'll wait too, half naked on the grass
until the Canada geese pull

me towards their breasts,

or the eggplants
—who are never far away—
call from their white flowers,
unbuttoning

the purple shades of black.

They turn their heads
from the dirt, closing
everything behind them
as though they have always known

where they were going.

IF BUILDING THE BRICK OVEN
IS WHAT SHE HAS DONE WITH HER LIFE

She bends
with the long wooden paddle,
reaching in

to its one room,
the bricks white, then orange,
then colors of wood and leather

as the day moves by them,
the bricks breathing
because she did not use mortar,

the bricks working
only as fast as the work.
She prepares the lamb sausages

and fresh tomatoes and cheese
and waits under a tree for the bread.
The oven is already older than she will ever be.

VIRGIL VISITS

He delights us with his fens and emmets,
farm knowledge, words from long ago.
He is curious about the arrowheads in this soil.
Beside us, in awe, he watches the bays and roans,
the whites and duns sweep the air with their manes,
the gadflies driving the whole herd crazy.

He shows us the burnt pungent galbanum,
the amellus in the meadow, silvery willow, spurge
laurel, fire-flush saffron, the lime blossom and rust-red martagon lily.
He takes us to the plough, stuck in the middle of the field
we never finished, to squills and hellebore and black bitumen,
shows us to put down spelt where we'd raised the brittle stalk

and rustling haulm of bitter lupin. Yes, Virgil
came to help us turn the fertile loam. In my dream it was so,
I held his hand and felt the words come through: holm-oak,
goose-grass and star-thistle, clover, trefoil.
He went to auction and helped us choose a cow
with shaggy ears under her crooked horns.

GRIEVING BY LEARNING THE LATIN NAME

The "silver dollars" my grandmother peeled and put into bouquets were part of a plant called *Lunaria annua*, a member of the mustard family. Towards the end of her life she began to gather them with a sense of urgency, peeling off the dried skins to reveal the shiny layer, the moon-wort, also called *honesty*. Her face shined silver. Her big, round glasses projected her squinting eyes while she fell asleep, the coins gathering in her arthritic hands, the coins falling into her lap. Was she trying just to keep busy, or did she want to barter each strange, translucent coin for one more day? Was she thinking: I will buy with the *Lunaria annua* one rising moon, one pale green egg, one sensation of water on my skin, one taste bud, one dog's dream in his twitching foot, one more Steven Foster song at the piano, one more silent movie soundtrack under Quabbin Reservoir, one more empty canvas, one more walk to the barn through the tracks of yesterday? Is this moon currency all that is left of the coins that paid for those silent movies, coins that paid for vegetables grown on the fields of Enfield when they were still fields?

EVERY TIME I HAVE NEVER BEEN HERE BEFORE

Dark beans
string their velvet tongues.
A horse eye blinks

through a curtain of mane,
purple the shake of black, black
the shade of sound. Nights

the nightshades undress and sing,
mares whip the air cantering.
The field reveals another node.

CIRCA THREE EARTH ACRES

Pasture, root sap, vole love.

An ebb of bees nicks the skins:

some moss, some blossom.

We weed the dewed weeds,

resume, measure the flecked calf,

the felt left in slow wools.

Ponies bend like spoons, bowing

to the pew of weeping willows, swallows.

Names emanate from traps

in their parted manes.

In the sow's house, slaw is the law of the walls, but

they are not dumb in their mud.

They nestle in. Listen.

THERE'S A LITURGICAL SOUND TO OUR NAMES FOR HER STOMACHS

On your knees again at the cow you ask each of them to grant you a wish. *Rumen*, you say, feed me the tomato garden through the window while I sleep. Let me smell the workhorses shift their weight by the basil, ready to comply. And let it be bareness that reveals. *Reticulum*, let me be alone all day on white ice under the white sky with vodka, like an ice fisherman in Labrador, waiting for the black crappies and bottle-green smelt. When nothing is happening, *omasum*, wake me up. Let me break the code of the frozen apple tree—before it drops anything. Four wishes are too many, you think, but already the *abomasum* is offering to help you suffer just enough that you will be shamelessly happy, unimportant, and master of the art of kneeling in the barn.

THE END OF MYTH

Dear Sisyphus, you don't have to roll
your stone any more. Let it go. Let it roll
down past the smaller stones, past shadows
of firs and all the sleepy birds you tried
never to wake, past that scent of foxes
that aroused you. There will be feasts,
there will be laughter, you can sit awhile
if you like, tell what you felt, driving
that weight like a workhorse along
the blackened river in the woods, along
the white lilacs that lowered their faces
in the rain. Tell of the monotony
of pine needles, and the porcupines
you knew were there on the mountain
but never saw, the train you heard
at the same moment you rolled
the stone through the wild thyme
and the scent rose and you thought,
so this, finally, is the breath.
Leave the stone that became your mother
and your father, your jug of wine,
your wound, your animal, your friend.
Let it roll down into the quiet valley and don't
watch it all the way until it stops.

MEMOIR OF A STONE

I was born broken and falling

and when I landed

two dragonflies landed on me

and mated.

I have grown smaller, going home,

down the backbone of the river

against other stones

who told their tales to each other

and imparted knowledge to the river

although they had no words or language

and their voices were not heard.

I warmed the bodies

of the boys lying on the riverbed,

I pushed their wet skin into their bones.

They listened to a radio, ate fruits

and drank some beer with a girl,

and when they went they left their bottles

but I will be here longer.

LOOKING AT COBB'S BARNS

From outside you suss out the timber frames.
A queen truss, arris fillets—no, just mortise
and tenon joints, joists of oak and hornbeam.

No more weathervane, though weather has changed
Venetian red to quinacridone rose—and in the sun
to raw umber and rose madder, even to the naked

tones of wood taken by rain, eaves not well hidden
under rows of cracked roofing shakes. The light
has rearranged the ridge, the verge and hem

into zinc white, golden green, manganese blue.
In each room an animal once slept and breathed,
the sleep braced by a stall and tucked stacks

of first cut hay, the breath braced by spider eggs
releasing legs into the rafters, then, and now,
and many evenings hereafter in South Truro.

"SURELY THE LEAST GLAMOROUS OF ALL PIGMENTS"

Dried corn stalks, weeds, cut hair.
Ripe under-leaves and trunks.
These blown burrs and branches have always been here,

late fall, Upstate.
The field-drab crops have been plowed under,
but muddied cattle still chew their cud, still

leave the cow-pie—and what is more lovely
than a fresh pasture-patty: tints that come of
taking in and giving back

broken down, simplified?
I will wear it. I will wave
to the beaver in the eddy by the old wooden bridge.

TAMWORTHS

Audrey says they weigh 230 pounds now, and they've been getting out every morning. They root in her Japanese eggplants and her ginger. They don't go far. She has begun measuring their girths, threatening them with the butcher. She says they are not cute anymore. When I dump the bushel of black hickory nuts into their pen they crack them open in their teeth, the sound a quiet in the clouds, a quiet in the ground, summer going, winter coming, this great compassion.

BUT I COULD NOT LET GO
OF WHAT I LONGED TO BE GONE FROM

When I walked down the road past the hard
black currants, beyond the smell of urine,
I said I would not miss this. I would not
miss the geese patrolling the yard, or the outhouse
that rose and sank. I would not miss the goats,
out of their fence, the goats eating the seat of my bicycle,
the goats bleating while I tried to listen to Edith Piaf
on a record, La Vie en Rose. I would not miss
my father, under the tractor, lit by a lamp,
my mother, shucking peas in the shade
of the shed where she'd hung skulls of sheep,
goat skulls, the small skull of a Holland Lop rabbit.
I would not miss the Highlands when they called out
in heat, informing the whole farm of their heavy longing,
or the old buck who rubbed his horn on the timber post
until the sack between his legs, a hanging world,
rested on bare dirt. I said I would not miss
the team of horses that had always come to the edge
of the field to meet me on my way home, one's mane
falling to the left, one's mane falling to the right, turning
their heads in unison. And when I reached the hill
on the far side of the valley and it had become winter,
I said I would never look back and I would never
imagine the oil lamps, still lit, or the snow
as it melted onto the animals' skins.

NEW YEAR'S EVE

Standing beside two draft mares at day's end:
they raised their heads and turned their eyes to me,
black, wet eyes like well bottoms that seemed to say:
you could adapt in this way too, if you would:
dark as the night, certain as the night
and broken in—with no sense of no home.

A barn cat sat beside me. He was lazy
as he washed one perfect paw, then the other,
and with me looked out to the two brown mares,
the smell of silage in the air and in his fur.
The team looked down and undid the first thrown bale,
chewing until we could feel the field cut free.

There as I listened I heard everything else
grow soft and of no use, and picked the cat
up into my arms and let his little heart
carry me, not off, but back to right here,
deeper in my shoes, deeper in my feet.
Let darkness, I thought, quench your tastes

and stay right here now. The darker horse
turned her head and breathed out long,
she rubbed her shoulder tight on her fairer sister,
then waited for a sign to change again,
the cat's voice somewhat deeper, satisfied
by warmth and two strings come loose on my jacket

that seemed to hold us there like slack reins
or baling twine, or bonds of left and right
that move this team with ease through woods, uphill,
backwards. The cold field held us for quite a while, too,
above, then inside the farm, as best it could,
with no hands, voiceless, ringing in decay.

WINTER SOLSTICE

The pail was bright, the teats were lit,

the hay still carried its hot summer evening.

Even the dull teeth of the bull gave off

a glimmer. In the farmhouse we told

stories on the way to sleep, of drunken

gold miners and a blind maiden

with no arms, eating pears in an orchard.

When the cat left we felt the darkest dark enter,

but already a distant flame in the coyotes' mouths,

under the fur, behind the lips, flickered

in the valley, and the tree that had fallen

in the woods glowed softly, full of honey.

The bees were reworking the comb.

The bees were flaring like matches.

WISHBONE

When my father's body enters this dirt
his team of horses will go in first, one
beside the other as they always have,
each still wearing the shoes he'd heated
and hammered with the anger he inherited—
beating it into the iron, not into his wife,
not into his three children. And every
fire poker, every candleholder will go in,
this nail and every nail and hammer.
The team will walk further, beyond
the cattle, beyond the birds, to a place where
the pulling away of horseshoes from hooves
will be like the pulling apart of a wishbone.
He will wish for more of the same:
more chickens carrying wishes, more
three-leafed clover, more horses, more
of this point where pulled grass
separates from its stalk, a horn rots
free of bone, the cow's back end opens
and one becomes two. And when his body
has dissolved into all the animals he drove
or ate—because his carnal hunger was also
hunger for the calm of animals he wanted
to become a part of his own flesh—the bell
will sound into the deepest empty cave
where fox cubs once chewed a slain fawn.
The valley will devour the bell's sound,
which has called and called these animals
home, and home will be all here, though
maybe there never was a farmhouse,
and maybe it was only ever the wall
of morning chores and the wall of evening
chores that held him; winter skins, summer.
There will be sky, and the floor will be
lovage and borage and a lost forest of elms.

LETTERS TO A FARM

To wait for your night by a kerosene flicker
while amber raspberries ripen in thickets
and fireflies light the marsh.
I have tried to want other things, to not desire
those endless summer fields.
But when I hold my ear to the ground
it is the peal of your sheep bells I hear.
Yours are the words I have held for years
in a wooden locket: fallow, shoats,
rumen, damselfly. Someday
I will run from this city.
I will stand at the door of your barn again,
washed by the hot full rain that follows
lightning, rain that has let go.
No matter how strange I may seem
I know you will say, *Come in.*
Listen to the cows. Sit on bales,
sit on bins. Come in,
come in and hold a kitten.

I will find the bones of buried pigs
and hang them on your clothesline,

listen to the sound of drying.

I will become a cattle egret who perches on the memory of cattle
and picks insects from the dark skins.
I will bury myself deep enough

goats' milk fills in
around my shoulders. Around my neck

I will wear a string of gourds and old farm machinery,

and in the ceremony
of your work

I will put coal on my ring finger
and tell myself: *wait.*
I will eat your apples

because apples are proof
and they have fallen from the trees.

Sometimes I will canter, sometimes walk
towards you. I will ride the mare, then the draft horses
who lift each hoof slowly over black sod,
whose shoes fall heavier than apples onto the road—
if there still is a road, and if there are horses,
the bridle, the halter, the girth. I will heed
the bare back, the silver mane. The crisscross path
is not just a moonlit, moss-lined dream.
I recognize home by the fiddleheads, the trumpet vine
turning orange in front of the farmhouse,
a soft breeze in the caps of oaks,
old salt licks still on the fields, like dice,
worn from too much wanting, too much looking
at the sky, too much thistle and ergot,
too many blowflies, breach births, and gnats.
I tuck my hands into your grain bins,
I balance on the haystack, hold a y-shaped twig
to divine all that once was, pulled down
by a warm pail of milk on the kitchen floor,
pulled down by a wet circle of sow
who surrenders her body to striped piglets.
They choke because there is always too much.
Even the tails of lambs are trimmed—I once kept one
secretly, held it nights in my narrow child's bed.
And where is it now, where is the dried
blue center of that cut that looked me in the eye
and said don't forget the storytellers, the hard pond
where you write the days' dates, where you mark
later swimming lanes. Don't forget the garden
that turns and opens like an always-healing wound.

I will go by banjo.
I will joke with distance like the Italian funambulist
who wore peach buckets on her feet
and walked backwards over Niagara Falls, blindfolded.
Every time I play a concert
the trumpet vine by your window will open,
your fiddleheads will unfurl.
I say I live in a city now, but my watch still moves to your rooster,
the udders, the thaws of your ground.
I have never answered a telephone without hoping to hear your nighttime cud.

Honeybees in late season
bring dust to the fronts of their hives,
sparrows turn straw sideways to fit holes in the barn,
the tongues of bells lie quiet next to sleeping sheep.
It has always been obvious to you
that all you have will also leave.
Is that because you are made of holes,
the swinging door, the winding road
where footprints fade and are filled with rain?
I have been walking, but not away from you.
I have tried to learn your gait.

The last carrot stays
in the dirt, a comma in the furrow.
Wait for the red fox, the earwig,
it says. Wait for the honeycomb.
That hill on the farm, it is your rye bread.
It is raining there, it is pouring milk.

NOTES

GOVERNED BY THE THRUMMING OF MY MOTHER'S SPINNING WHEEL:
In Jonathan Bate's biography of John Clare, Clare is quoted: "I measured this
ballad today wi the thrumming of my mothers wheel—if it be tincturd wi
the drone of that domestic music you will excuse it after this confession."

**THE DAY EMILY DICKINSON HELPED MY FATHER BUILD A SMALL HOUSE
IN VERMONT:** The italicized material is from poem 124 by Emily Dickinson,
beginning "Safe in their Alabaster Chambers—."

VIRGIL VISITS: Some of the language in this poem is taken directly
from Virgil's *Georgics*, books 3-4, translated by A.S. Kline.

THERE'S A LITURGICAL SOUND TO OUR NAMES FOR HER STOMACHS:
The title is taken from a passage in Kristin Kimball's *The Dirty Life:
A Memoir of Farming, Food, and Love.*

LOOKING AT *COBB'S BARNS*: *Cobb's Barns and Distant Houses* is a
painting by Edward Hopper.

"SURELY THE LEAST GLAMOROUS OF ALL PIGMENTS": The quotation
refers to a statement from *Bright Earth: The Invention of Colour*, by
Philip Ball.

BUT I COULD NOT LET GO OF WHAT I LONGED TO BE GONE FROM:
The title is part of a line from W.S. Merwin's poem, "Completion,"
in *The Vixen*.

ABOUT THE AUTHOR

Molly Bashaw grew up on small farms in Massachusetts, upstate New York, and Vermont. She studied at the Eastman School of Music before working for twelve years in Germany as a professional bass-trombonist. In 2012-13 she served as the George Bennett Fellow writer-in-residence at Phillips Exeter Academy, and is currently attending graduate school in Germany. Her poetry has been awarded the Lynda Hull Memorial Prize, the River Styx International Poetry Prize, a scholarship at the Bread Loaf Writers' Conference, and a Pushcart nomination. This is her first book.

ABOUT THE ARTIST

Kathleen Laraia McLaughlin is a photographer and educator with an appetite for exploring the world. For her efforts at capturing a disappearing world, she has received a Fulbright Senior Scholarship, IREX IARO Grant (from the National Endowment for the Humanities), and a Houston Center for Photography Fellowship for her work in Romania. Her images have appeared in *PDN*, *LensWork*, *Rangefinder*, *B&W Magazine*, *Black + White Photography* (UK), and *The Times Saturday Magazine* (UK). Her photographs have been exhibited both nationally and internationally and are in the permanent collections at the Museum of Photographic Art in San Diego, Western Virginia Museum of Art, and the U.S. Embassy in Bucharest. She received her MFA in Photography from Virginia Commonwealth University.

ABOUT THE WASHINGTON PRIZE

The Whole Field Still Moving Inside It is the winner of the 2013 Washington Prize. Molly Bashaw's collection was selected from among 324 manuscripts submitted by American and Canadian poets.

READERS: First readers were Barbara Anderson, Stuart Bartow, George Drew, Michael Gossett, Jonathan Hall, Elaine Handley, Erich Hintze, Amy MacClennan, Marilyn McCabe, Kathleen McCoy, Michael Mlekoday, Yvonne Murphy, Cat Richardson, Naftali Rottenstreich, and Mary Sanders Shartle. Second readers were Carrie Bennett, Brad Richard, Jay Rogoff, Barbara Louise Ungar, and Maria van Beuren.

FINAL JUDGES: Karren Alenier, J.H. Beall, Barbara Goldberg, Leslie McGrath, and Nancy White

OTHER WASHINGTON PRIZE BOOKS

Nathalie F. Anderson, *Following Fred Astaire*, 1998
Michael Atkinson, *One Hundred Children Waiting for a Train*, 2001
Carrie Bennett, *biography of water*, 2004
Peter Blair, *Last Heat*, 1999
John Bradley, *Love-in-Idleness*, 1989, 2nd edition as eBook 2014
Richard Carr, *Ace*, 2008
B. K. Fischer, *St. Rage's Vault*, 2012
Ann Rae Jonas, *A Diamond Is Hard but Not Tough*, 1997
Frannie Lindsay, *Mayweed*, 2009
Richard Lyons, *Fleur Carnivore*, 2005
Fred Marchant, *Tipping Point*, 1993, 2nd edition 2013
Ron Mohring, *Survivable World*, 2003
Brad Richard, *Motion Studies*, 2010
Jay Rogoff, *The Cutoff*, 1994
Prartho Sereno, *Call from Paris*, 2007, 2nd edition 2014
Enid Shomer, *Stalking the Florida Panther*, 1987, 2nd printing 1993
John Surowiecki, *The Hat City after Men Stopped Wearing Hats*, 2006
Miles Waggener, *Phoenix Suites*, 2002
Mike White, *How to Make a Bird with Two Hands*, 2011
Nancy White, *Sun, Moon, Salt*, 1992, 2nd edition 2010

ABOUT THE WORD WORKS

The Word Works, a nonprofit literary organization, publishes contemporary poetry and presents public programs. Since 1981, it has sponsored the Washington Prize, a monetary award and book publication for an American or Canadian poet. Other imprints include The Hilary Tham Capital Collection, International Editions, and, starting in 2014, The Tenth Gate.

Monthly, The Word Works offers free literary programs in the Chevy Chase, MD, Café Muse series, and each summer, it holds free poetry programs in Washington, DC's Rock Creek Park. Annually in June, two high school students debut in the Joaquin Miller Poetry Series as winners of the Jacklyn Potter Young Poets Competition. Since 1974, Word Works programs have included: "In the Shadow of the Capitol," a symposium and archival project on the African American intellectual community in segregated Washington, DC; the Gunston Arts Center Poetry Series (featuring Ai, Carolyn Forché, and Stanley Kunitz); the Poet Editor panel discussions at The Writer's Center (including John Hollander, Maurice English, Anthony Hecht, Josephine Jacobsen); and Master Class workshops (with Agha Shahid Ali, Thomas Lux, Marilyn Nelson).

As a 501(c)3 organization, The Word Works has received awards from the National Endowment for the Arts, the National Endowment for the Humanities, the DC Commission on the Arts & Humanities, the Witter Bynner Foundation, Poets & Writers, The Writer's Center, Bell Atlantic, the David G. Taft Foundation, and others, including many generous private patrons. The Word Works has established an archive of artistic and administrative materials in the Washington Writing archive housed in the George Washington University Gelman Library. The Word Works is a member of the Council of Literary Magazines and Presses and distributed by Small Press Distribution.

More information at WordWorksBooks.org.

Other Available Word Works Books

FROM THE HILARY THAM CAPITAL COLLECTION

Mel Belin, *Flesh That Was Chrysalis*
Doris Brody, *Judging the Distance*
Sarah Browning, *Whiskey in the Garden of Eden*
Grace Cavalieri, *Pinecrest Rest Home*
Christopher Conlon, *Gilbert and Garbo in Love* and
        Mary Falls: Requiem for Mrs. Surratt
Donna Denizé, *Broken like Job*
W. Perry Epes, *Nothing Happened*
Bernadette Geyer, *The Scabbard of Her Throat*
Barbara G. S. Hagerty, *Twinzilla*
James Hopkins, *Eight Pale Women*
Brandon Johnson, *Love's Skin*
Marilyn McCabe, *Perpetual Motion*
Judith McCombs, *The Habit of Fire*
Miles David Moore, *The Bears of Paris* and *Rollercoaster*
Kathi Morrison-Taylor, *By the Nest*
Tera Vale Ragan, *Reading the Ground*
Maria Terrone, *The Bodies We Were Loaned*
Hilary Tham, *Bad Names for Women* and *Counting*
Barbara Louise Ungar, *Charlotte Brontë, You Ruined My Life*
Jonathan Vaile, *Blue Cowboy*
Rosemary Winslow, *Green Bodies*
Michele Wolf, *Immersion*

INTERNATIONAL EDITIONS

Yoko Danno & James C. Hopkins, *The Blue Door*
Moshe Dor, Barbara Goldberg, Giora Leshem, eds., *The Stones Remember*
Moshe Dor (Barbara Goldberg, trans.), *Scorched by the Sun*
Lee Sang (Myong-Hee Kim, trans.), *Crow's Eye View: The Infamy of
        Lee Sang, Korean Poet*
Vladimir Levchev (Henry Taylor, trans.), *Black Book of the
        Endangered Species*

ADDITIONAL TITLES

Karren L. Alenier, *Wandering on the Outside*

Karren L. Alenier, Hilary Tham, Miles David Moore, eds.,
  Winners: A Retrospective of the Washington Prize

Christopher Bursk, ed., *Cool Fire*

Barbara Goldberg, *Berta Broadfoot and Pepin the Short*

Jacklyn Potter, Dwaine Rieves, Gary Stein, eds.,
  Cabin Fever: Poets at Joaquin Miller's Cabin

Robert Sargent, *Aspects of a Southern Story* and *A Woman From Memphis*

CPSIA information can be obtained at www.ICGtesting.com
Printed in the USA
BVOW04s0609060214

343971BV00003B/3/P